How to Competitively Price Your Product or Service

The most effective methods for pricing your product

Table of Contents

Everything You Need to Know About Pricing

If you are going to sell something on the Internet, the single most crucial decision you will make is how to price your services/products. Because the Internet provides customers with thousands of alternatives, you must keep up with the competition. How long you can stay in the market will be determined by the pricing you accept.

You should have a firm grasp on pricing. How far can you push it? How often should the prices be reviewed? Much will be determined by how you approach this stage of the process.

To begin, you must choose a consumer group and estimate how much they are willing to pay for your services or products.

However, you must also ensure that you make a profit. And these two requirements are frequently at odds. Different people utilize various strategies to set their product prices. Some have a scientific basis, while others do not. One such approach is described below, and it requires an awareness of the manufacturing cost, customer expectations, and other players in the field.

Cost is defined as the sum of all expenses incurred when producing a product. Expenses include the cost of raw materials, machinery, packaging, and shipping, among other things. The price is the amount that buyers must pay per unit of your goods or service.

To make a profit, your pricing should be higher than your cost. Except in exceptional circumstances, your pricing should be continuously higher than the cost if you intend to run your business for a long period. Prices can sometimes be reduced to gain access into a market, for example. People will notice you if you start with prices that are cheaper than your competition. And once you've amassed a sizable customer base, you may progressively raise your prices

Customers' willingness to pay for your services is proportionate to how significant and valuable they believe your product is. Of course, your marketing methods and market reputation will be important factors in this regard.

Your optimal pricing is found between these two numbers, your cost and the price your buyers are willing to pay for your product. If you set your price a little lower than what your consumers are prepared to pay for your services, it will undoubtedly benefit you in the long term.

If your price is more than what is reasonable in the eyes of the customer, you will lose attractiveness, market share, and eventually viability.

Working with Price-Conscious Buyers

In today's society, the worth of money is a stark reality, which is why clients looking to shop for their requirements are mindful of the cash component when purchasing.

They want to get the most bang for their buck, which is why properly pricing your items goes a long way toward ensuring that you keep receiving customers and making profits. However, this does not imply that you can just entice clients by lowering prices, as this can sometimes result in losses.

However, the worth of the goods, rather than the price, determines its price in the eyes of the client. A high-profile vehicle, such as a Mercedes, will never be priced in line with the rates of a Toyota, but they will demand the best bargain from you when looking to buy a Toyota in the market.

Thus, giving value to any product through smart marketing, research, and development is a definite approach to ensure that your customers appreciate and agree on the price and worth of the product. As a result, it is simply a matter of modifying the way a buyer perceives a thing.

The easiest and most effective technique for satisfying a price sensitive buyer is to paint a vivid picture of the long-term rewards of their purchase. Everyone wants to know that their money was well spent on something that will last and provide them more money in the future. So, if you can persuade the client that purchasing something is about investing in something important and long-term, they would gladly part with the money.

You may just be able to close the deal by demonstrating how the more expensive item would ultimately cause fewer difficulties and hence save a lot of effort and wasteful money on servicing and repairs. This is all about convincing clients that they are making the right decision by considering the long-term benefits of the purchase.

Any sensible buyer would come to you if you have a quality product and market it successfully. Customers want the best in the market for themselves, even if it means spending an extra penny. As a result, providing high-quality products never fails to entice customers to return for more.

To win over price-sensitive buyers, you must first recognize that price is not the only factor influencing their purchasing decisions. You will be able to showcase the entire value of your service or consumer if you take the time to unearth their demands. If you fail to unearth the full picture, you may find yourself answering price worries, which will not help your firm prosper in the long run.

So, get to know your clients. Determine how their thoughts function and what they desire. This will go a long way toward convincing and enticing customers to purchase the proper, if costly, goods. If you don't understand that buying is about more than just money, but also about all of the other factors described above, you might have to continually lowering your pricing to attract clients, which isn't very beneficial for your business.

How to Get the "Winning Price"

Setting a pricing for your goods or service, particularly when selling on the Internet, can be the most important business choice you make. Setting a price is more difficult than it appears. If you want to earn a profit, your price should be more than your cost but less than the 'price the market can bear,' which is the price your consumers expect to pay for your service. When pricing your products, keep these considerations in mind.

There are complex price plans that you must comprehend and operate with. The pricing plan you choose will be determined by your business strategy.

Such as the 'Pricing to Penetrate' strategy. This strategy would be appropriate if your goal is to swiftly reach the target market. To reach this goal, you must set a cheap price for your goods.

However, it is critical to determine how low you can go before hitting rock bottom. You must determine the lowest you can go without incurring debts and suffering significant losses. You should not be concerned about incurring initial losses if it means gaining long-term consumers.

But how can you determine a customer's lifetime value?

Keep your loyal clients and take steps to keep them loyal to your company. If you want to leave a lasting impact, penetration pricing is useful. It can also be effective in situations where several new companies are entering the market.

Your product should be the ultimate "sticky product" that the buyer cannot live without. Online brokers, for example, are so much more convenient that once a person is hooked, they don't even consider alternatives.

Manufacturing a great product is another strategy to ensure customer retention. When selling books online, for example, a superb book at a reasonable price can secure your immediate success.

Because of their significantly subsidized pricing, Amazon.com is the dominant player among online book sellers. Despite the fact that this business strategy may have cost them thousands of dollars, they have managed to build a stable customer base on which they can now rely.

Another real-world example is how razor manufacturers realized that reselling razor blades rather than handles would be far more profitable, and the rest, as they say, is history.

Pricing Depends on the Product Type

Finding the proper price for your product is critical to long-term and short-term success. The correct pricing for your goods is somewhere between the cost and the price a consumer is willing to pay for your services. The cost would include raw material expenses as well as other fixed and variable manufacturing expenses.

So much so that it has the potential to double or triple your profits. Technically, your products will fall under one of two categories:

Commodity: There is a lot of competition in this industry because the products of the different participants are the same; it's just the price that they compete on. You must be razor sharp and always on your toes. The only things that will set you apart are your proficiency and efficiency. Things will get messed up again if you are too relaxed.

Propriety goods: These are genuine goods. Genuine and unique in their own right. You compete with the other market participants based on the unique strengths of your offerings. If you're skilled enough and in demand, you can establish a pricing that ensures you make the most money.

The Internet market is rapidly evolving. To stay competitive, you may need to change your rates periodically due to new competition and changes in demand, among other things.

Then there are things that are both common and proprietary, such as computer hardware. Computer systems are continually being upgraded and become more sophisticated, and competition is fierce. It is a proprietary product in the sense that a Macintosh can still afford to be significantly more expensive than a standard Windows system due to the additional functionality it provides.

In any case, you can't afford to price your goods incorrectly because it will imply rapid death in the market.

Price wars are a regular occurrence for any firm in this day and age. To survive, you must always be on your toes and deliver on your promises. If one rival cuts his pricing, everyone else must follow suit. But if you don't, you should have plenty of reasons to stick to your guns. One good reason is a strong customer base that will stick with you no matter what.

Profitable Pricing Strategies

Pricing tactics are an often-overlooked component of the marketing mix. They can have a significant impact on earnings and should be given the same consideration as marketing and advertising techniques. A price increase or decrease can have a significant impact on gross margins and sales volume. This indirectly affects other expenses by, for example, lowering storage costs or opening up options for volume discounts with suppliers.

Other considerations will also influence your best pricing strategy. Consider the five elements that impact other company decisions: your competitors, your suppliers, the availability of substitute products, and your customers. Positioning how you want to be seen by your target audience is also an important factor. Customers will not believe the quality of a premium item if it is priced too cheap, for example. Customers will buy lower-priced items from competitors if the selling price on value lines is too high.

Consider the following pricing strategies:

- Reasonable pricing
  The greatest way to conduct business is to keep your prices competitive. Keep an eye on how much your next-door competition is charging for their products and then price yours similarly or less than theirs.

- Price plus markup
  The polar opposite of the previous strategy, this one seeks to set your prices according to your preferences, based on the profit percentage you want to keep rather than the market. However, while this has the advantage of winning you a lot of money by setting low pricing, it may also work against you in some scenarios. So, before deciding on a price, think carefully.

- **The Loss Leader**

  Another effective method for attracting customers and increasing sales is to sell relatively inexpensive items at a reduced price to customers who have the potential to purchase more expensive stuff. However, this is a transient arrangement that is frequently a gamble.

- **Finish up**

  This is an intriguing strategy to explore while emptying up your inventory. This strategy entails selling your excess goods at incredibly low prices in order to avoid losses.

- **Trade discounts or membership**

  Understand your customers. Shortlist the ones who can make you money and provide them exceptional deals so that they are enticed to buy more from you and continue to return. So lower your rates, offer discounts, and do whatever it takes to entice customers back into your store.

- **Volume and bundle discounts**

  The simple one plus one free method also works well. So provide a significant discount to chosen clients on large purchases of the same kind, such as 5 shirts, or comparable or related things. To avoid losses, make offers on old product or combine one new with one old to clear out excess inventory.

- **Versioning**

  Putting several versions of the same basic product together and then giving cheaper pricing for the more basic models is a good strategy to not just get rid of those models to the typical person. However, one can combine offers such as free servicing for a limited time with higher cost ones to work as an incentive for high purchasing clients.

So, go ahead and employ these strategies to get the level of earnings you've always sought.

Pricing Strategy: Price Skimming

One of the most significant marketing methods you will apply in your organization is the pricing plan. Along with selecting the proper product, smart marketing, and a solid sales strategy, the right price strategy will determine your revenues and market share. Market skimming is a pricing tactic commonly used by industry leaders.

A computer company's plan is to release a new laptop every 8 months or so. He reduces the price of older, unsold models (which are in their maturing stage) while maintaining the price of new laptops (which are in their initial stage). The new laptops will be more expensive due to their improved functionality.

As a result, the manufacturer is skimming the price (or skimming the market) during several stages, including introduction, growth, maturity, and decline. He makes the most profit by charging the greatest fee for each of these levels.

This strategy will operate in a large market with a significant number of buyers, a high product or service demand, and a low-cost structure for the organization. In the preceding example of laptops, demand is high, and there are many repeat purchasers in an industry with a low-cost structure that is technologically enabled.

The company's current problem stems from the fact that there are a large number of competitors in this sector. If all of these competitors offer a whole range of similar products, each with a different life cycle, purchasers will have a very difficult time judging the product in terms of quality, service, or value for money.

In the face of a slew of similar-looking devices, the consumer will opt for the laptop with the most features at the lowest price. And if your company does not have the lowest price, it may harm its brand reputation because it would appear as if you have been overpricing things, resulting in a reduction in sales.

Before deciding on a pricing plan, make sure you thoroughly research the market. One should have a clear notion of how customers will behave and how competitors would act or react. And, if the market conditions change, this strategy should be assessed on an ongoing basis to ensure that the factors that led to it have not changed.

Is Psychological Pricing a Successful Marketing Strategy?

The word "price" has a psychological value. Buyers believe that if a thing is expensive, it must be greater valuable. Despite the fact that this idea is based on psychology rather than truth, it makes price tangibles more effective than the product itself.

However, it is interesting to note that as the customer becomes more familiar with the nature of the goods, his decisions become more rational, and higher price ceases to be the measuring rod for product value. One prominent example of psychological pricing is that customers prefer prices that end in odd numbers, such as $9, $99, because they believe they are getting a better deal than if the prices ended in even numbers, such as $20, $66, and so on.

If the objects to be priced are in a price "band," as in online auctions, or in an odd range figure, such as $199,00, the products will be judged more valuable than a $200,00 listing. The psychology behind such consumer behavior is that prices in an out of the ordinary range are frequently regarded as a better bargain. As a result, it is critical to ensure that you have chosen the appropriate price and strategy for the product.

Reference pricing is another example of psychological pricing. When purchasers attach to a price psychologically, it immediately reflects their perception of a product's relationship to its price. Reference pricing is very significant in the case of high-value products such as luxury items, and a whole firm can be funded on this premise.

However, one must exercise caution when positioning prices because the tactic may backfire if the customer believes the product does not belong in that category. If the product contains attributes that appeal to an ego-conscious buyer, reference pricing is an appropriate price strategy.

High-end luxury things that appeal to ego-sensitive buyers are one example of this. To be effective with reference pricing, you must guarantee that the price you have decided for a product fits it best from all perspectives and viewpoints, including your own.

Before releasing the product to the target market, ensure that the chosen pricing fits the product and has been tested. The impact of numerous market elements on the price tag must also be considered. The product must be appropriate for a psychological pricing strategy, the promotional program must be adequate for the pricing strategy, and the distribution channels must be in sync with the price and not outperform the product's cost.

Pricing for Market Penetration

Market penetration pricing is a quick-entry pricing technique that assumes that when a product is priced low, sales volume increase, lowering total costs. This is a helpful tactic for price-sensitive markets. Consider the DVD player market; not only are sales volumes huge, but so are the number of competitors.

DVD player production costs have plummeted, and constantly improving technology has allowed for the rapid introduction of new features and benefits on new models. Companies that profit from DVD players and sell in large quantities at low or fair costs are all pursuing a market penetration strategy.

Market penetration pricing is typically used by entrepreneurs to try to grow a market for their brand while also penetrating the market for the product as a whole. All estimates assume that the lowest price will obtain the most market share. However, before using this pricing approach, it is critical to first assess your market, price sensitivity, and price elasticity or in-elasticity.

A certain degree of market research is also required in order to understand and predict how your competitors will react to this cutting-edge pricing strategy. For example, if your cheap price causes your opponent to decrease his price as well, this will result in a dead end since you will then drop your price again, provoking a similar reaction from him, and so on until no one wins.

While the preceding statement is correct, it is also true that your market penetration price plan may only serve as a disincentive to prospective competitors considering joining the market. The chance of a new entrant gaining a substantial market share is really high, and when they consider how cheap your price is, they will see that their margin will be poor, therefore they may opt not to enter the market due to the risks.

However, in order to be successful with this technique, you must be willing to take advantage of the economies of scale that big sales volume brings, as well as be the market's lowest-cost provider.

If you already have a business and your opponent is pursuing a market penetration plan, you must conduct the same extensive market research and evaluation of your own capabilities:

• Is it possible for you to cut your expenses?

• Are you confident that it will create large quantities?

• Are you willing to accept the risk of selling your product at a low price in the expectation that volume sales would result in the market share and profitability you seek?

If you answered no to any of these questions, think twice before using this penetration approach, and if you're still not convinced, don't do it.

However, if you are a new business owner exploring this strategy in a new or sparsely populated industry with little competition, focus on ways to reduce your costs and increase your efficiencies.

Whatever pricing method you choose, make sure you include it in your marketing mix plan, along with the reasoning for your decision.

At the time of your yearly business plan update, evaluate your chosen marketing approach, including your pricing strategy, to ensure it is the best strategy for your product in light of market conditions, consumers, and rivals.

Special Offers

When releasing a new product, promotional pricing is typically used. It is used to boost demand for products that have a lagging demand. Price target buyers are typically those looking for a bargain. Some of these promotional event pricing examples are intended for special occasions. These are typically intended for certain occasions such as Christmas or Easter.

There are rebate schemes or allowances available when purchasing a home. Sometimes the seller will offer a move-in fee, carpet replacement allowance, renovation allowance, or a refund for all cash with no difficulty financing or purchasing large items such as cars. Many stores may advertise no-interest financing options for their furniture purchases.

These pricing plans are also available at car dealerships for previous year models. These sales methods have been incredibly successful, but you must be cautious when employing them because clients are growing increasingly sensitive to the genuine value of the strategies. Another phase method that appears to be effective is purchase one, get one free or get two for the price of one.

This is conceivable if the product cost is cheap, the profit margin is healthy, and there is an excess of inventory. Another important way of payment is the prolonged payment term.

You must pay a deposit and make payments over time. Only once you pay will you be able to obtain the product. This is highly frequent in the renovation and building industry because the payment is made first as the initial cost, then when the job is halfway finished, and finally when it is completed.

Sometimes a low-cost warranty or no-cost warranty can help with these business initiatives. A good product usually has no returns and a satisfied consumer. As a result, these techniques have a good influence. Customer distrust has resulted from the overuse of these techniques. They look for the truth in the transaction. The "going out of business" sale is the most common type of promotional pricing.

This sale may be deceptive or misleading. It is a relocation of the same company. You should be conscious as a consumer that you are not being tricked into such a plan. There are still many effective promotional price plans available, so choose your pricing methods wisely.

Pricing That is Competitive

Do what your customer does to determine whether your things are priced too expensive or not. Look it up on the internet. According to a 2006 yahoo!/OMD survey, approximately 66% of families use the Internet to conduct product research, and 64% use the search engine to purchase a product.

Look up any of your products on the Internet. Compare your prices to those of others; this will help you sell more. It is as simple as typing the name and asking for a pricing comparison. It may take some time depending on the goods you sell and the market saturation. This would provide valuable insight into your firm and make you aware of what you are up against.

You might be able to differentiate your product and persuade your buyer to buy from you. Begin by lowering your costs. This is always beneficial. If you notice an opportunity to cut your pricing further, take advantage of it. Your item will become the "lowest price ever on the web!". Low cost encourages buying, which compensates for the price disparity.

Ensure a price match. Inform your customers that you will match any price and will not be undersold. Once the consumer arrives, make them complete the purchase. You could also provide them with free shipping. If your item is more expensive than the competitor's, you might offer free delivery to give your item the lowest cost at checkout.

Any purchaser will appreciate the free shipping offer. This term has a significant impact on whether or not you make the sale. If you lose a customer, it will be because the customer is not convinced by the price of the goods. To persuade your buyer that your product is worth the money and absolutely worth acquiring from you, you must make certain improvements.

Cost is not the only element influencing purchase, but it is one of the most important. So, if you have offered your customers the best buy in terms of product value, you will have an advantage over the rest of the rivals.

Including Discounts in Your Pricing Strategy

It is tough to price goods. There is no single determinant magic formula that can determine the best pricing for a product. There is no simple solution, but certain steps can be taken to create more efficient pricing practices. Pricing selections are tough to make because one can only rely on one's own judgment. Even so, decisions are never entirely satisfying.

The determination of the pricing of goods or services is one of the most important in business. Product pricing must be done in such a way that the intended customers are willing to pay that amount while still generating profit for the company, or else the business will fail.

Pricing can be approached in both scientific and non-scientific ways. The framework for pricing decisions presented below considers your costs, the consequences of competition, and the customer's impression of value.

As part of marketing, pricing policies are occasionally overlooked.

They can have a significant impact on earnings and should be given the same consideration as marketing and advertising techniques. Price changes have a significant impact on both gross margins and sales volume. This has an indirect influence on other expenses by, for example, lowering storage costs or opening up options for volume discounts with suppliers.

Your pricing plan may include discounts to customers who provide you with a competitive edge.

Customers that pay on time may be eligible for monetary discounts. As a result, this method compensates those who assist a company in maintaining a consistent, positive cash flow and lowering credit-collection costs.

When the cost-per-unit to sell or deliver a product decreases as the quantity increases, quantity discounts for large orders make economic sense. A caterer, for example, may fill an order for 12 dozen cupcakes for one customer at 10 cents each, whereas cupcakes sitting on the bakery display rack may be sold to numerous customers at 20 cents each throughout the day.

This is done because the possibility that some of the cupcakes will not sell must be taken into account. The costs of keeping the store open for the convenience of random consumers are also included. There are costs associated with having the store open for the convenience of random customers.

Seasonal reductions reward customers who help a business balance its cash flow and satisfy production goals.

Trade-in allowances for returned used products that can be re-used or re-sold for a profit benefit both the company and the consumer.

Promotional allowances are frequently economically sound. For example, if your product is used in advertising or promotional activities by a retail chain that also sells your product, your marketing efforts will benefit. If this is the case, you may wish to provide a price reduction to the retail chain that does so.

Pricing Options

Pricing is without a doubt one of the most significant aspects of any marketing mix strategy. Correct pricing can make or break your goods in the market. The following elements must be considered when promoting your product:

- It must be of superior quality

- It must have features that your buyers require or desire

- It must be different from what your competitors offer

- It must have a good cost structure

- You must also pay attention to a strong promotional campaign

- With these factors in mind, it is critical to determine the pricing strategy in a way that allows you to successfully sell your product in the market.

Some different pricing techniques are listed below:

1. **Generic or Economic Pricing:** The buyer is drawn to this tactic by the low price. It's common of generic or low-cost brands. To make this method work, you should have a low-cost structure, few features, and lots of promotion. Concurrently, ensuring that you receive some real, consistent benefits.

2. **Differential pricing:** The idea behind this method is to set the price based on different buyer types (for example, an online store, a retail store, and a department store); geographical area (prices can be higher in California than in Illinois); quantity purchased (a person buying large quantities will get a different rate than someone buying a small quantity); and national account segment (the price charged to a national account will vary from that charged to a local account). Remember that there must be a valid rationale for using differential pricing.

3. **Premium pricing:** This method is appropriate for high-end or luxury items such as pricey jewelry, yachts, jets, estates, and so on. If the market sees your product as a luxury or premium item, you can employ this method.

4. **Pricing for captive products or companion products:** This method can also be used to product line pricing. Products are grouped together as companions in this situation and priced accordingly. (For example, a mixer and a mixing bowl). They also regard items as slaves (e.g. a razor that can only be fitted with a particular blade). These items are frequently packaged together. (For example, razor blades may be packaged with the razor.) The prices of these products when purchased separately are frequently greater.

Remember to carefully examine your products before deciding on a strategy to ensure that the cost is reasonable.

Change Your Prices to Make Your Offerings More Appealing in Ways Other Than Price

The days of men swearing by Gillette and ladies looking no further than Guerlain are long gone. In the global market, monopolies are rare, and every product has a competitor, a substitute that is continuously seeking to outperform the other. Price is the most typical basis for competition in such multi-product markets.

Typically, buyers are drawn to things that are less expensive to purchase than its counterpart. Because differentiated items predominate, overall quality is roughly the same.

From the producer's perspective, the only way to reduce his product price is to reduce his costs. However, production procedures cannot be altered without affecting quality. And, of course, if one has to cut costs, the quality is bound to suffer as well. Another option would be to boost production scale. However, this takes time. As a result, another measure is required for immediate effect.

Block pricing is a common pricing technique used by supermarkets and wholesalers. When a consumer sees a sign that states, "Milk- 1 gallon $3.00; 4 gallons $10.00," he instantly concludes that he is saving money by spending two dollars less if he purchases it in quantity.

As a result, task accomplished. Although buying things in bulk appears to save consumers money, his spending habits would be different if he had 1 gallon of milk instead of 4 at a time.

Intelligent offers are another technique to catch the buyer's attention. The concept of FREE is well understood by all. It's a small word, yet it has a great impact.

Conditioners are typically purchased together shampoos, scrubs alongside soaps, and socks alongside shoes. As a result, if a large bottle of shampoo comes with a tiny bottle of conditioner for free, this could entice more purchasers.

Buffets in restaurants charge a set price per person. This means that someone who orders soup, chicken a la Kiev, and dessert pays the same as someone who orders only the chicken and dessert. This may appear to be unjust to person 1, but no one ever refused to offer him soup.

As a result, while pricing is a consideration, it is primarily a psychological war in which the buyer is presented with numerous options from which to pick.

Pricing Based on Value

Pricing a product based on its perceived worth is critical. Customer preferences, product benefits, corporate image, ease, and product quality are all subjective characteristics that will assist an organization in understanding the customer's impression of the value of its product or service.What customers want is critical.

Are they saving money or time by acquiring your product? Is there a competitive advantage that they receive by using your service? What options do they have? Is it more convenient for them to use your service than of doing it themselves? What exactly does the competition require?

If the preceding points are kept in mind, the maximum price the client will pay for the advantage gained can be understood.

Several value-based pricing schemes are listed below. They consider the break-even point as well as subjective judgements.

1. **Setting the same price as competitors** - This is utilized when pricing for a commodity product are normally well-established (such as professional services) or when there are no other options for setting prices. The goal, then, is to figure out how to reduce expenses in order to earn bigger profits than competitors.

2. **Setting a Low Price** - This is done primarily to catch a huge number of buyers in the market in question. This method is also used to achieve non-financial goals such as meeting the competition, creating a low-cost image, or just increasing product awareness. If profitability can be maintained at the low price, or if sales levels are acceptable, this method succeeds and can eventually lead to price increases.

3. **Charging a high price** - It is possible to charge a high price relative to the cost of the product if it is distinctive and useful to buyers. The target market's wealth also matters. In such a circumstance, positioning a product as a "prestige

product" allows for a high price to be charged. Rolex watches, for example, may not have such a high manufacture cost. However, the high price provides a "status" benefit to the rich Rolex market.

Charging customers what they are "willing to pay," even if it is a high price, is a strategy that needs vigilance and judgment. It also necessitates a readiness to adapt because customers (as well as competitors) may determine that the profits are excessive. As a result, a variety of factors influence value-based pricing, but an astute strategy may make the most of it.

How Do You Know If Your Pricing Is Correct?

Even if you have the best product/service in the world, if your prices aren't perfect, you won't get anywhere. POPS, CAPS, AND VAPS are the three basic pricing techniques used by Internet companies. They can only assist firms obtain an advantage over the competition if they are properly applied.

(POPS) Tangible OBJECT PRICING STRATEGY, which works well by selling a physical item as well as one that is shipped to your clients. This category includes Amazon.com and Wal-Mart. These companies begin by determining the cost of producing and delivering one additional product to establish the price. (This is known as the marginal cost).

Consider the case of Wall-Mart. They have microwave ovens for sale. How much would it cost them to sell one additional unit? To figure this amount, they would need to know how much they pay their suppliers, how much they pay to place it in the store, and how much they pay to complete their transaction. To establish the ultimate price, a company must add the marginal cost.

The operating profit margin is as follows:

To determine the proportion, they must compare it to similar other firms. Amazon's profit margin is 6%. Competing merchants should aim for the same operating margin, preferably a smaller one. A company that develops an efficient business process can save costs and help them keep their prices low while maintaining an attractive margin.

COST OF ACQUISITION PRICING STRATEGY (CAPS). POPS works successfully if your primary cost is the real cost of the goods you are delivering. Firms supplying products/services where the cost is marketing-based, such as the number of visitors to your website, may benefit from using CAPS to decide their final price. CAPS often responds to two important questions.

1. How much will it cost to encourage people to visit a website?

2. What is the percentage of site visitors who will make a purchase?

To calculate the firm's cost per acquisition, divide the answer to the first question by the response to the second question. As a result, the operational profit margin can be added to this to get the ultimate price.

For example, a merchant may discover that a visitor to the site costs $0.10 on average, with 1% of visitors making a purchase. So we simply calculate the cost per acquisition from here. And we figure out what the final cost should be. The aim here is to keep the cost per acquisition as low as possible..

VALUE ADDED PRICING STRATEGY (VAPS). For firms where the marginal cost is zero, such as the selling of digital products such as e-books and online courses. VAPS function well when developing a company plan that allows you to charge different prices to different clients.